THE OLYMPICS

MODERN OLYMPIC GAMES

HAYDN MIDDLETON

The Olympic Spirit

The modern Olympic Games began in 1896. Since then the Games' organizers have tried to ensure that every competitor keeps to the true Olympic spirit. This spirit is based on fair play, international friendship, a love of sport purely for its own sake, and the ideal that it is more important to take part than to win.

Heinemann Library
Chicago, Illinois

© 2000 Reed Educational & Professional Publishing
Published by Heinemann Library,
an imprint of Reed Educational & Professional Publishing,
Chicago, IL

Customer Service 888-454-2279
Visit our website at www.heinemannlibrary.com

Designed by AMR
Printed in Hong Kong/China

04 03 02 01
10 9 8 7 6 5 4 3

Library of Congress Cataloging-in-Publication Data
Middleton, Haydn.
    Modern Olympic games / Haydn Middleton.
        p. cm. – (Olympics)
    Summary: Explores the development of the modern Olympic games from
    their inception in 1896, discussing location, logistics, rituals,
    events, and who is allowed to participate.
    ISBN 1-57572-453-7 (library binding)
    1. Olympic Juvenile literature. [1. Olympics.] I. Title.
II. Series: Middleton, Haydn. Olympics.
GV721.53.M56 1999
    796.48—dc21   99-24273
                                                   CIP

Acknowledgments
The Publishers would like to thank the following for permission to reproduce
photographs: Allsport, pp. 4, 6, 7, 8, 9, 11 (left), 12, 13, 14, 15, 17, 18, 19, 20, 22, 24, 25,
26, 27; Colorsport, pp. 11 (right), 23, 28, 29; Corbis/Nik Wheeler, p. 16; Michael Holford,
p. 5.

Cover photograph reproduced with permission of Sporting Pictures (UK) Ltd.

Every effort has been made to contact copyright holders of any material reproduced in
this book. Any omissions will be rectified in subsequent printings if notice is given to the
Publisher.

Any words appearing in the text in bold, **like this**, are explained in the
Glossary.

Contents

Introduction

The Olympic Games are the most important international athletic competition in the world. Every four years they bring together thousands of the world's best athletes to compete in an ever-growing number of individual and team sports. Millions of spectators have attended the Games and marveled at the astounding performances. Over a billion TV viewers worldwide tune in and share in the excitement as it happens.

This book tells the story of how the Olympic Games began and how they developed into the competition we know today.

Games like no other

Since the first modern Games in 1896, the Olympics have been held in twenty-one different countries on four different continents. And since 1924, there have been separate Winter Olympics, as well as Summer Olympics. Countless athletes from all over the world have focused their hopes, dreams, and talents on taking part in these Games. All have hoped to achieve the ultimate success— winning an Olympic gold medal. Few have fulfilled this ambition, but no one who competes at the Olympic Games ever forgets the experience.

Each Olympic Games has its own atmosphere and flavor, depending on where it is held. Yet every Games has traditional rituals and ceremonies that make the occasion uniquely Olympic.

"I do not know why man likes sport," wrote American author Ed Wheeler in a book written for the Atlanta Olympic Games in 1996. "Maybe for the same reason that the dog tosses his bone. Is it a statement of possession, amusement, or boredom? The Olympics are, or could be, the highest expression of sport. The Olympics test our bonds to Earth and lift the fact that we are alive."

At times the Games have faced serious political crises. On several occasions, during major wars, they have not been held. People have often predicted a complete end to the Games, because of the difficulty and expense of organizing them. Yet they have not only survived, they have grown in popularity and scale. The Millennium Games, held in Sydney, Australia, in the year 2000, will feature more competitors than any previous Games.

Olympic origins

Although the modern Games began in 1896, they were not the first Olympics ever. For those, you have to go back almost 3,000 years to ancient Greece. The five-day-long Games held then featured running, combat sports, the **pentathlon**, horseback riding, and chariot races.

There are records of winners dating back to 776 B.C., but the ancient Games came to an end in A.D. 393 when the Roman Emperor, Theodosius I, banned all non-Christian worship throughout his empire. Since the Olympics were held in honor of the Greek gods, they had to come to an end as well. But just over 1,500 years later, the Games began again in their modern form.

This ancient Greek vase painting shows the old Greek sport of *pankration*, an aggressive one-on-one combat sport.

Bring Back the Games!

By the end of the 19th century, many people in Europe and America were interested in sports. Some might even have dreamed of a brand new global Games based on the ancient Greek Olympics. But one man above all others made this dream come true. His name was Pierre de Fredi, Baron de Coubertin. He was a French **aristocrat** who loved sports, even though he was not particularly good at them!

A religion of sport

De Coubertin (1863–1937) was a widely traveled man. In Britain he saw how important sports were in the **public schools**. In the United States he admired the highly-developed training and coaching programs at the colleges. Sports became a kind of religion to him, as expressed in what he said and wrote about it.

Baron Pierre de Coubertin was the father of the modern Olympic Games.

Through sports, de Coubertin said, "our body rises above its animal nature." Sporting contests, he believed, are "the means of bringing to perfection the strong and hopeful youth. . . helping towards the perfection of all human society."

"Sport," he concluded, "should allow man to know himself, to control himself, and to conquer himself."

In 1892, he started trying to convert others to his strong faith in sports. His aim was to set up some games where the youth of the world could come together in peaceful, character-building competition—a modern Olympics. It was especially important to him that everyone taking part should be an **amateur**. The athlete's reward would not be money; it would be the glory of being an Olympian.

Birth of an Olympic family

At first, de Coubertin found little support for his grand idea. Then in June 1894, at a meeting in Paris, he persuaded **delegates** from twelve countries to back his plan to revive the Olympics. The Games would be held in Athens, the capital of Greece, in 1896. Then, at four-year intervals, other major cities would serve as hosts for the Games. Soon more countries came into this new "Olympic family," and an International Olympic Committee (IOC) was organized to oversee the Games. De Coubertin served as chairman of the IOC for 30 years.

The first modern Olympic Games were held in Athens over ten days in June 1896. An estimated 245 men—most of them Greek—took part in 43 events. Few of the performances were very good. In fact, in events such as the discus and long jump, champions from ancient times probably achieved greater distances! But the Games were hugely popular with the large crowds that came to watch. The world's appetite was whetted for more sport.

This was the official program of the 1896 Games. Athletes from fourteen different nations took part.

Article 46 of the Olympic Charter states that the Olympic Games are not competitions between nations. They are contests between individuals and teams. But ever since 1896, nations have competed against one another to gain the most success.

7

The Games Roll On: 1900-1936

			COMPETITORS		NATIONS	EVENTS
			Men	Women		
II	1900 Paris, France	May 20–Oct. 28	1,206	19	26	87
III	1904 St. Louis, Missouri	July 1–Nov. 23	681	6	13	94
IV	1908 London, England	Apr. 27–Oct. 31	1,999	36	22	109
V	1912 Stockholm, Sweden	June 29–July 22	2,490	57	28	102
VI	1916 Berlin, Germany	Canceled due to World War I				
VII	1920 Antwerp, Belgium	Apr. 20–Sept. 12	2,591	78	29	154
VIII	1924 Paris, France	May 4–July 27	2,956	136	44	126
IX	1928 Amsterdam, Netherlands	May 17–Aug. 12	2,724	290	46	109
X	1932 Los Angeles, California	July 30–Aug. 14	1,281	127	37	116
XI	1936 Berlin, Germany	Aug. 1–16	3,738	328	49	129

The table above shows how the Olympic story continued in the 40 years after 1896. Until 1932, the Games lasted for months. Now, they take just two weeks. The early Games weren't just long, they were very disorganized as well. Some competitors were not even aware that the event they were taking part in was part of the Olympic Games. Sometimes, too, **professional** athletes were allowed to compete.

Slowly but surely, organization improved, and there were fewer disputes over which events were official and which were not. The fifth Games at Stockholm set a new standard for efficiency, but then the 1916 Games were canceled, because of World War I. In ancient Greece, not even war could stop the Games. Instead, a **truce** was declared to let the athletes travel to the Games and compete in safety.

This official Olympic poster advertises the 1912 Games, the first Games in which athletes from five continents took part.

OLYMPIC GAMES STOCKHOLM 1912 JUNE 29 th — JULY 22 nd.

Games between wars

The Olympics resumed in 1920. The Games were held in Belgium, which had suffered horribly during World War I. "All this is quite nice," remarked King Albert I of Belgium at the opening ceremony, "but it certainly lacks people." The 1924 Games in Paris had bigger crowds, but trouble kept breaking out because the fans were so aggressive in their support. This was definitely not in the "Olympic spirit."

The men's 4 × 400-meter relay at the Berlin Olympics of 1936 was the first event to be shown on television. Berliners could watch the Games for free on giant screens in the city theaters.

Women participated in **track and field** events for the first time at the 1928 Games in Amsterdam. Before then, they had taken part in tennis, golf, archery, figure skating, yachting, and fencing. At the next Games in 1932 in Los Angeles, fewer women and men competed. This was partly because it was too expensive for many Europeans to travel to the United States.

Also, making and selling alcohol was illegal in the United States at that time. But the athletes from France and Italy were allowed to drink wine, because they said it was a vital part of their diet.

In 1931 the International Olympic Committee decided to stage the eleventh Games in Germany. Two years later Hitler and his **Nazi** Party came to power. Despite much protest, the 1936 Games went ahead in Berlin. As a spectacle they were lavish, since Hitler wanted to prove the supremacy of the German people. Hitler's influence over the Olympic story extended beyond 1936, because the next two Games, in 1940 and 1944, were canceled due to World War II.

Truly Global Olympics: 1948–1968

		COMPETITORS		NATIONS	EVENTS
		Men	Women		
XII and XIII 1940 and 1944	Canceled due to World War II				
XIV 1948 London, England	July 29–Aug. 14	3,714	385	59	136
XV 1952 Helsinki, Finland	July 19–Aug. 3	4,407	518	69	149
XVI 1956 Melbourne, Australia	Nov. 22–Dec. 8	2,958	384	72	151
XVII 1960 Rome, Italy	Aug. 25–Sept. 11	4,738	610	83	150
XVIII 1964 Tokyo, Japan	October 10–24	4,457	683	93	163
XIX 1968 Mexico City, Mexico	October 12–27	4,750	781	112	172

During the 20 years from 1948 to 1968, more and more nations took part in the Olympics. The number of events grew, too, until in 1968 there were 172 sporting events ranging from **track and field** to **equestrianism** to yachting and to shooting. Each Games produced outstanding performances and fantastic champions, whose names became known all around the world. But there were troubles, too, partly because the Games could not remain entirely separate from world events.

War by other means

The British did a good job as hosts of the 1948 Games in the wake of World War II. The defeated countries, Germany and Japan, were not invited to take part, just as the defeated countries of World War I were kept out of the 1920 Games. Some countries that had recently become **communist** sent teams to compete. From this moment on, rivalry between communist and noncommunist nations would be a major feature of the Olympic Games.

The most powerful communist nation of all, the Soviet Union (**USSR**), joined the Olympics for the highly exciting 1952 Games in Finland. Afterwards, the official Soviet newspaper claimed that the USSR had "won" the Games and exhibited the superiority of Soviet athletes. The USSR's great **Cold War** rival, the United States, responded by saying that the U.S. athletes had "won."

Broader horizons

In 1956, the Olympics were first staged in the southern hemisphere. Several nations, including Egypt, Iraq, the Netherlands, and Spain, refused to send teams to these Games in Melbourne, Australia. That was their way of showing disapproval at political or military aggression carried out by other competing nations. There were to be more **boycotts** in the future. The International Olympic Committee (IOC) banned South Africa from taking part in the 1960 Games in Rome. The exclusion was a punishment for the South African government's brutal treatment of nonwhite people. The ban lasted for 32 years, until the segregation system of **apartheid** ended.

The Games then made a debut in Asia when Tokyo hosted the 1964 Games, with great success. But there were fierce disputes when the IOC announced Mexico City as the site for 1968. Mexico City is more than 6,500 feet (2,000 meters) above sea level, and according to one Danish newspaper, "At least half a year is needed to adapt to the oxygen-poor air. One's life would be endangered trying to break records." In the Mexico City Games, records were broken and no one died. Another controversy arose when female athletes were asked to take gender tests. Some competitors were suspected of using chemicals to improve their bodies, which in effect made them more male than female.

The photos show two Olympic opening ceremonies: London in 1948, and the spectacular ceremony in Tokyo in 1964.

Towards 2000: The Games Since 1972

			COMPETITORS		NATIONS	EVENTS
			Men	Women		
XX	1972 Munich, West Germany	Aug. 26–Sept. 10	6,065	1,058	121	195
XXI	1976 Montreal, Canada	July 17–Aug. 1	4,781	1,247	92	198
XXII	1980 Moscow, USSR	July 19–Aug. 3	4,092	1,125	80	203
XXIII	1984 Los Angeles, California	July 28–Aug. 12	5,230	1,567	140	221
XXIV	1988 Seoul, South Korea	Sept. 17–Oct. 2	6,279	2,186	159	237
XXV	1992 Barcelona, Spain	July 24–Aug. 9	6,659	2,708	169	257
XXVI	1996 Atlanta, Georgia	July 19–Aug. 4	6,797	3,513	197	271

At the first Games in 1896, sportsmen from fourteen nations took part. A century later at the Atlanta Games, men and women from almost 200 nations competed. The Olympic motto is "swifter, higher, stronger," but when it came to being the host for the Games, the motto could have been changed to "big, tough, extravagant." The Germans spent $30 million to stage the 1936 Games. When the Olympics returned to Germany in 1972, they cost almost 70 times that amount. Although those Games were a great sporting success, disaster struck when Palestinian **terrorists** caused the deaths of eleven Israeli athletes.

The 1976 Games in Canada were hit with two problems. First, many African nations stayed away because the New Zealand rugby team had competed against the banned South Africans. Second, through bad planning, the Games proved very expensive to the Montreal **taxpayers**.

A tremendous stadium complex was built for the 1972 Olympic Games at Munich.

More world records were broken at the 1980 Games in Moscow than four years earlier in Montreal, but even fewer nations sent teams. This was due to the biggest-ever Olympic **boycott**, led by the United States. It included 64 other nations in protest of the **USSR's** invasion of Afghanistan in 1979. Four years later the USSR led a smaller boycott of sixteen nations for the 1984 Games in Los Angeles, California. Reasons for not participating included complaints about security and **commercialization**, although many felt that it was retaliation for the 1980 boycott. For the first time since 1896, private individuals, not taxpayers, were organizing and paying for the 1984 Games. Huge sums of money were raised by selling TV rights, tickets, and commercial sponsorships. This time there would be no danger of another Montreal-style financial fiasco.

The Millennium beckons

In 1988 the Olympic spotlight shifted to Asia. The 1988 Games were held in Seoul, South Korea, the "Land of Morning Calm." The peaceful efficiency of these Games was scarred by only a small boycott. Of greater concern for the Olympic movement was the disqualification of ten athletes for their illegal use of drugs. Three of those athletes were gold medalists.

The 1992 and 1996 Games were nearly free of trouble, except, tragically, for a terrorist bomb that killed two people and injured over 100 others in Atlanta, Georgia.

The 27th Olympic Games, held in Sydney, Australia, in the year 2000, will have the greatest number of athletes ever to compete. These Millennium Games will probably be the biggest ever. More than 1.3 million visitors are expected to attend.

Olympic champion boxer Muhammad Ali lights the Olympic flame at Atlanta in 1996. The opening ceremony was watched by billions of viewers worldwide.

Who Gets the Games?

It has always been a great honor to be the host for the Olympic Games. It has also been a very complicated and increasingly expensive business to stage them. Greece, the host country of the first modern Games in 1896, wanted the Games to be held there permanently. This suggestion was made again in the 1980s, since organizing each new Games had become so costly for the host cities.

Both times, the International Olympic Committee (IOC) said no to the one-site suggestion, because the Olympic Games are truly international and should be held all over the world. In addition, a Games held in a city such as Tokyo has a very different feel and flavor than one held in Mexico City.

Presidents of the International Olympic Committee

1894–96	Demetrius Vikelas (Greece)
1896–1925	Baron Pierre de Coubertin (France)
1925–42	Count Henri de Baillet-Latour (Belgium)
1946–52	J. Sigfrid Edstrom (Sweden)
1952–72	Avery Brundage (United States)
1972–80	Lord Killanin (Ireland)
1980–	Juan Antonio Samaranch (Spain)

The IOC's early rules said that the IOC President should be from the next nation to host the Games. Since Paris was to be the host of the 1900 Games, de Coubertin got the job in 1896. But then he was persuaded to stay in office until 1925. After that he became honorary president until his death in 1937. The IOC, based in Lausanne, Switzerland, is the ruling body of the Olympic Movement. It works closely with the International Federations (IFs) that govern individual Olympic sports and the National Olympic Committees (NOCs) of individual countries. The IOC also chooses the organizing committees, which, every four years, make sure that the Games run smoothly and fairly.

The Olympic Charter

The Olympic Charter is the official set of rules for the Olympic Movement. It says that some of the IOC's aims are "to encourage the organization and development of sports and sports competitions; . . . to fight against any form of discrimination affecting the Olympic Movement; to lead the fight against doping in sport; . . . and to see to it that the Olympic Games are held in conditions that demonstrate a responsible concern for environmental issues."

Bidding for the Games

Host cities need a long time to prepare for the Games. As early as September 1993, Sydney, Australia, was given the go-ahead to hold the Games in the year 2000. But its bid, or Olympic plan, had to face stiff competition from other big cities.

The IOC has to think carefully about many factors before deciding which bid will be successful. Sydney's bid was helped by the fact that no Games had been held in the southern hemisphere since 1956 and that it has no history of **terrorism**. The bid also made a commitment to hold "Green Games." As part of its ecologically sensitive preparations, Homebush Bay, a neglected **landfill** site that was once called the most polluted place in Australia, is being **reclaimed**. Also, when a rare colony of green and golden bellfrogs was discovered in the area planned for the Olympic tennis courts, the plans were changed and the tennis courts moved elsewhere.

In 1993 these delegates celebrated their winning bid to hold the 2000 Olympics in their home city of Sydney, Australia.

In 1999 a scandal was revealed. Several cities, including Salt Lake City, Utah, and Sydney, had bribed IOC officials to vote for their bids. A major investigation followed in an attempt to clean up the bidding process and to restore the good name of the IOC.

This Olympic stadium at Sydney, Australia, is part of the site of the 27th Games for the year 2000.

Global Village

A tidal wave of competitors and team officials will arrive in Sydney for the 27th Games in the year 2000. Where will they all stay? The city's organizing committee claims that for the first time in modern Olympic history, they will all live in one Olympic Village and will be able to walk to their events.

Village or mini-city?

At the earliest modern Games, athletes and officials made do with whatever accommodations they could find. The American team of 1912 stayed on board the ship that had brought them across the ocean to Stockholm. Competitors in Antwerp in

1920 lived in the city's schools and slept eight to a classroom.

But at the Los Angeles Games of 1932, the first special Olympic Village was built. It was more like a mini-city with its own post office, hospital, fire station, and security guards. The guards had instructions not to admit women. There were only 127 female competitors, and they all stayed in a Los Angeles hotel. A village was also built for the Berlin Games of 1936. At Helsinki in 1952, there were two villages because the **USSR**-led **communist** countries demanded separate, secure quarters for their competitors. This was partly in fear that their athletes might **defect** to western countries.

This photograph shows part of the Olympic Village for the 1996 Games in Atlanta, Georgia. These Olympics were called the largest peacetime social event in human history.

The building of more recent Olympic Villages has helped make host cities better places for their own citizens. In order to build a village for the Barcelona Games of 1992, a stretch of the waterfront was **reclaimed** and developed. Then, after the Games, local people moved into the specially built low-rise apartments.

The design of the Village for the 2000 Games in Sydney is extremely **eco-friendly**. It features solar street lighting and the recycling of waste water for garden irrigation. "As the 2000 Games are the first major event of the next century," say the organizers, "it is fitting that the Olympic Movement leads the push to protect the environment."

By 1992 **professional** players were allowed to take part in many Olympic events. The United States' basketball "Dream Team" at the Barcelona Games was led by Magic Johnson. Eleven team members were multimillionaire NBA stars. Being such superstars, they bypassed the Olympic Village and stayed in $900-a-night hotel suites elsewhere in Barcelona.

Village life

Judo silver medalist Nicola Fairbrother lived in the Olympic Village at Barcelona in 1992. "You can taste the apprehension in the air, sense the hopes and the dreams," she wrote. "All the food in the Village was free. You could eat when, and as much as you liked. Soon the main food hall became like a magnet for socializing.

"I also have vivid memories of the atmosphere as I walked about the Village. It was like a bond that existed through every competitor in the Village, regardless of color, size, shape, or sport. You could watch African runners lope by, followed by a group of tiny, Hungarian gymnasts and the Chinese volleyball team. There would be the same look in all of their faces. Everyone in the Village seemed united by the incredible experience. Everyone seemed *alive*."

The Marathon: Ancient Meets Modern

The longest Olympic race is the marathon. It has been a highlight of the men's events in all the modern Games. Since 1984 there has been a women's marathon, too. The idea for the race came from an old Greek legend. In 490 B.C. the Greeks won a famous victory over the Persians at the Battle of Marathon. It was said that Pheidippides, a **professional** runner, ran the enormous distance of about 25 miles (40 kilometers) back to Athens to break the good news. "Rejoice, we conquer!" he declared on arriving, and then died of exhaustion. Whether the story is true or not, the organizers of the 1896 Games in Athens decided to hold a long-distance race named for the great Greek Battle of Marathon.

Local hero

The first Olympic marathon was 25 miles (40 kilometers) long. Although it was run mainly on roads outside Athens, it would finish in the Olympic stadium. To the joy of the huge crowd waiting there, the first man home was a local farmer, Spiridon Louis. He finished in a time of 2 hours 58 minutes 50 seconds. It was Greece's only victory at the Games. Local merchants tried to shower Louis with gifts. All he accepted was a horse and cart to transport water to his village.

Spiridon Louis was the first Olympic marathon winner in 1896. Forty years later, the German Olympic Organizing Committee brought him to Berlin for the 1936 Games. He presented to German leader Adolf Hitler a laurel wreath from the sacred grove at Olympia, which was the site of the ancient Olympics. Spiridon Louis died in 1940.

Memorable marathon moments

The marathon has rarely been short of drama. In 1904, in St. Louis, Missouri, Zulu tribesman Lentauw (one of the first two black Africans to compete in the Olympics) was chased off course and through a cornfield by dogs. He still finished ninth.

The 1908 London marathon began at Windsor Castle and ended in the Olympic stadium, a distance of 26 miles. Then the runners had to push themselves through another 385 yards around the track so that the finish line would be right in front of Queen Alexandra's royal box. In all but two of the Games since then, the official marathon distance has been set at 26 miles 385 yards (about 42 kilometers).

In 1960 Rome held the first night marathon, because it was too hot to run during the daytime. Both that race and the 1964 marathon were won by Ethiopian Abebe Bikila.

In the 1972 Munich marathon, the first man into the stadium was Frank Shorter of the United States. He was surprised to hear booing instead of cheering, but the booing was not for him. Just before he entered the stadium, a person posing as a runner had appeared on the track and run a full lap before security guards caught him. The crowd was jeering the imposter.

In Barcelona in 1992, Mongolian Pyambuu Tuul recorded a time of 4 hours 44 seconds, the slowest time in 84 years. Tuul had been blinded by an explosion in 1978. Then in 1990 he ran in the New York marathon with the help of a guide. A year later an operation gave him partial sight, so he entered the Barcelona Olympics. He said he was there not to win, but "to show that a man has many possibilities."

The winner of the third women's marathon, run in Barcelona in 1992, was Russia's Valentina Yegorova. A thirty-year-old TV set was moved into the street of her small hometown, so that hundreds of her friends and neighbors could crowd around to watch her win the gold.

Which Sports?

How many different Olympic sports are there? It can be tempting to think only of **track and field**, gymnastics, and swimming. Those sports certainly attract more media coverage than most, but they are just the tip of the iceberg. At the 26th Olympic Games in Atlanta, Georgia, the competitors took part in 271 different events. World-class facilities are provided for all the sports, making it a big job for the host city to hold the Olympic Games.

Summer Olympic sports in Atlanta, Georgia—1996

Archery
Badminton
Baseball
Basketball
Boxing
Canoeing/Kayaking
Cycling
Equestrianism
Fencing

Field Hockey
Gymnastics
Judo
Modern **Pentathlon**
Rowing
Shooting
Soccer
Softball
Swimming and Diving

Table Tennis
Team Handball
Tennis
Track and Field
Volleyball
Water Polo
Weightlifting
Wrestling
Yachting

At Sydney in the year 2000, there will be two more sports—Triathlon and Tae kwon do.

Canoeing is a fiercely contested Olympic sport. Kayak events feature paddles with a blade at each end. The paddles in Canadian canoeing have only one blade.

The International Olympic Committee's Program Commission constantly discusses the Olympic sports that already exist and the possibility of adding new ones. Some sports fans around the world were not sure if beach volleyball was a serious enough sport to be added to the events in Atlanta. At various Games since 1896, many sports have tried and failed to find a permanent place in the Olympics. Some sports now belong only to the Olympic past.

Discontinued Olympic sports

(The date tells when the sport was an Olympic event.)
Cricket (1900) Britain won over a French team of mostly Englishmen.

Croquet (1900) France won all three croquet events.

Golf (1900, 1904) In 1904 Canadian golfer (and practical joker) George Lyon became an Olympic champion and accepted a silver trophy by walking to the ceremony on his hands!

Jeu de Paume – "Real Tennis" (1908) Jay Gould of the United States won the gold.

Lacrosse (1904, 1908) In 1908, when Frank Dixon of Canada broke his stick, British opponent R. G. W. Martin offered to withdraw from the game until a new one was found. The Canadians went on to win the Olympic finals.

Motorboating (1908) Britain's Thomas Thornycroft won gold in two different classes. Forty-four years later, at age 70, he was selected for the British yachting team for the 1952 Helsinki Games.

Polo (1900, 1908, 1920, 1924, 1936) In the last competition, Argentina won the gold in front of a crowd of 45,000 people.

Racquets (1908) Britain won a clean sweep of all the medals.

Roque (1904) hard-surface croquet. A clean sweep for the United States.

Rugby (1900, 1908, 1920, 1924) Team member Daniel Carroll won gold for Australia in 1908 and then again for the Unites States in 1920. No one else has ever won gold medals for representing different countries.

Tug-of-war (1900, 1904, 1908, 1912, 1920) The first team to pull the opposing team for six feet was declared the winner. In 1908 teams of British policemen came in first, second, and third.

Olympic Rituals

Processions and parades took place at the ancient Greek Games and now they are dramatic features of the modern Olympics. Each new opening ceremony is watched by huge TV audiences and seems to outdo the one before it for spectacular entertainment and effect. The procession of competitors is still led by Greece, followed by all the other national teams in alphabetical order. The host country's team appears last. In Melbourne in 1956, a seventeen-year-old Chinese boy suggested that everyone should walk together as a single **multicultural** nation at the Games' closing ceremony. It made a wonderful sight.

In Barcelona, Spain, in 1992, a crowd of 100,000 people and a TV audience of two billion watched one of the most breathtaking opening ceremonies ever.

The Olympic oath

"In the name of all competitors, I promise that we will take part in these Olympic Games, respecting and abiding by the rules that govern them, in the true spirit of sportsmanship, for the glory of sport, and the honor of our teams."

Since 1920, a representative of the host country has taken this oath at the opening ceremony of the Games. Usually the representative is a veteran of previous Games, such as Finnish gymnast Heikki Savolainen at Helsinki in 1952 and Korean basketball player Hur Jae at Seoul in 1988.

Mascots

The first Olympic mascot made its appearance in Mexico City in 1968. The mascot was a red jaguar. Since then each Games has had its own mascot, which usually has some connection with the host country. Popular mascots have included Waldi the Dachshund at Munich in 1972, Misha the Bear at Moscow in 1980, and Cobi the Dog at Barcelona in 1992. Since 1980 the Winter Games have had mascots, too.

Tending the flame

The Olympic flame was first lit at Amsterdam in 1928. It burned throughout the Games. Eight years later, the Olympic torch was ignited in Olympia, Greece, by the sun's rays. Then 3,000 relay runners brought the sacred fire 1,800 miles (3,000 kilometers) from Greece to Berlin. In 1956, for the Melbourne Games, the torch traveled for the first time by airplane. Twenty years later, the flame's energy sent a laser beam from Greece to Montreal to light an identical torch. Then in Atlanta in 1996, there was a moving moment when Olympic champion boxer Muhammad Ali lit the Olympic flame in his own country.

Since 1920 this has been the official Olympic flag. It was designed by the founder of the modern Games, Baron de Coubertin. The colored rings are believed to represent the five populated continents of the world. They are linked together by sports. These five colors were chosen because, in 1920, at least one of the colors appeared in the flag of each participating country.

Medal ceremonies

In ancient Greece, all the Olympic winners were presented with olive wreaths at the end of the Games. At each modern Games until 1928, victory medals were also given out at the closing ceremony. Now medals are presented to the winners of each event as it takes place. Olympic gold medals are 90 percent solid silver with 1/5 of an ounce (6 grams) of gold on the outside.

The podium or victory stand, with its first, second, and third positions, was introduced in 1932. Some people think national anthems should not be played at Olympic medal presentations, because the Games are meant to be international. At Tokyo in 1964, when Abebe Bikila received Ethiopia's first gold medal, the Japanese band did not know the Ethiopian national anthem, so it played the Japanese anthem instead.

Men Only?

In ancient times very few women were allowed to watch Olympic events. No women were allowed to take part. When the modern Games began in 1896, there were still no women competitors. Many people believed that women's bodies could not cope with the demands of top-level sport. Some thought, too, that a woman's true place was in the home, not the stadium.

Times change, and so do people's ideas. The number of female Olympians has increased over the past 100 years, until in 1996 in Atlanta, 3,513 women took part. That figure is still short of the 6,797 male participants, but the gap is closing all the time.

Women admitted at last

The earliest female Olympians were golfers and tennis players. Margaret Abbott of the United States won a golfing gold medal at a Paris tournament in 1900 without realizing that she was participating in the Olympic Games!

COMPETITORS AT THE SUMMER OLYMPICS			
Year	Olympic City	Men	Women
1896	Athens	245	–
1900	Paris	1,206	19
1904	St. Louis	681	6
1908	London	1,999	36
1912	Stockholm	2,490	57
1920	Antwerp	2,591	78
1924	Paris	2,956	136
1928	Amsterdam	2,724	290
1932	Los Angeles	1,281	127
1936	Berlin	3,738	328
1948	London	3,714	385
1952	Helsinki	4,407	518
1956	Melbourne	2,958	384
1960	Rome	4,738	610
1964	Tokyo	4,457	683
1968	Mexico City	4,750	781
1972	Munich	6,065	1,058
1976	Montreal	4,781	1,247
1980	Moscow	4,092	1,125
1984	Los Angeles	5,230	1,567
1988	Seoul	6,279	2,186
1992	Barcelona	6,659	2,708
1996	Atlanta	6,797	3,513

The first Olympic marathon race for women was held in Los Angeles in 1984. It was won by Joan Benoit of the United States in a time of 2 hours 24 minutes 52 seconds. That was an improvement over the first official, pre-Olympic time for a female marathon runner of 3 hours 40 minutes 22 seconds by Violet Piercy of Great Britain in 1926.

Women made their debut in Olympic **track and field** events at Amsterdam in 1928. For the first time women competed in the 100-meter run, the 400-meter run, the discus, and high jump. They also took part in the 800-meter run, but several runners were seen to be "in distress" at the end of a difficult race. It was another 44 years before a longer women's race, the 1,500-meter run, was added to the events. It was not until 1984 that women were allowed to compete in the most grueling Olympic race of all—the marathon.

A woman called Babe

One woman who did more than most for the cause of female Olympians was Mildred "Babe" Didrikson. At the Los Angeles Games in 1932, this confident eighteen-year-old American announced, "I came out here to beat everybody in sight, and that is exactly what I'm going to do." She proceeded to win the javelin throw and break the world record to win the 80-meter hurdles. In the high jump, she tied for first place and claimed another world record, but received only a silver medal because an official called her head-first diving style illegal. She would have won more gold medals, but women were allowed to compete in only three events. Babe had qualified for five. In later life she excelled in basketball and golf. Someone once asked if there was anything she did not play. "Yeah," she replied, "dolls."

Babe Didrikson was the heroine of the 1932 Olympics.

For the Love of Sport

Amateurs are meant to play sports purely for the love of it. **Professionals** receive material rewards. These days almost all Olympic competitors are professionals—even professional tennis and basketball stars take part. Sporting standards are so high that few athletes could train to the highest level and still hold regular jobs. Yet that was what the organizers of the first modern Games wanted athletes to do. And until quite recent times, amateurism remained the Olympic ideal.

A noble tradition

"The important thing in the Olympic Games is not winning, but taking part. The essential thing in life is not conquering, but fighting well." Baron de Coubertin and his fellow organizers of the first modern Games believed very strongly in this point of view. For them, simply taking part was its own reward. There was no question of money being paid, either as a prize for the winners, or to reimburse competitors for their training expenses. Olympic sport was thus a glorious hobby for those who could afford to take part.

But the line between amateur and professional in Olympic sports was never completely clear. Spiridon Louis won the first marathon in 1896 and received a simple laurel wreath for his achievement. But his fans also promised him a multitude of gifts, including free groceries, free travel, and free haircuts for life. Material rewards such as these sometimes went to the victors.

Competing in sports these days can be expensive. Business sponsorship can help pay the costs of equipment, training, and traveling to competitions.

Olympic athletes were once meant to be amateurs. But by 1974 National Olympic Committees were allowed to pay athletes who trained full-time, and in 1981, **track and field** athletes were allowed to receive money to endorse products, such as running shoes.

Paralympic progress

In the first part of the modern Olympic era, there was no place for physically challenged competitors who loved sports. This seemed unfortunate to Sir Ludwig Guttman. He became the founder of the Paralympics.

In 1948 Guttman was director of the National Spinal Injuries Center at Stoke Mandeville Hospital in England. His original idea was to hold competitive sports for people with spinal injuries at the Stoke Mandeville Games. But year by year people with other disabilities and from other nations got involved. In 1960 a "parallel Olympics" for handicapped men and women began. In that year 400 athletes competed in Rome. By 1996, in Atlanta, the number was closer to 4,000. The Paralympic Games are now usually held during the ten days or so following the Olympic Games.

Sports at the Paralympics in recent years range from table tennis to baseball to basketball to team rhythmic gymnastics. After the Barcelona Games, the British *Sunday Times* reported, "The stadium was on several occasions packed with up to 55,000 people who had not come to be 'nice to the disabled' . . . but to see athletics of the highest caliber."

At the Barcelona Paralympics in 1992, Tanni Grey from Wales won four gold medals in the 100-meter, 200-meter, 400-meter, and 800-meter races. This achievement is surpassed only by Bart Dodson of the United States.

Ice-Cold Olympics

There was figure skating in the Olympic Games of 1908 and 1920. Ice hockey was played in 1920. But in 1924 the International Olympic Committee established a completely separate Winter Olympic Games. From then until 1992, the Winter Olympic Games were always held the same year as the Summer Games, although not always in the same country. Beginning with the 1994 Games in Lillehammer, Norway, the Winter Olympics were rescheduled to take place in the even-numbered years that fell between the Summer Games.

In the 1924 Games at St. Moritz, there were fourteen events in five different sports. At Nagano in 1998 there were 67 events, including curling and women's ice hockey.

THE WINTER OLYMPICS
1924 Chamonix, France
1928 St. Moritz, Switzerland
1932 Lake Placid, New York
1936 Garmisch-Partenkirchen, Germany
1948 St. Moritz, Switzerland
1952 Oslo, Norway
1956 Cortina, Italy
1960 Squaw Valley, California
1964 Innsbruck, Austria
1968 Grenoble, France
1972 Sapporo, Japan
1976 Innsbruck, Austria
1980 Lake Placid, New York
1984 Sarajevo, Yugoslavia (now Bosnia)
1988 Calgary, Canada
1992 Albertville, France
1994 Lillehammer, Norway
1998 Nagano, Japan
2002 Salt Lake City, Utah

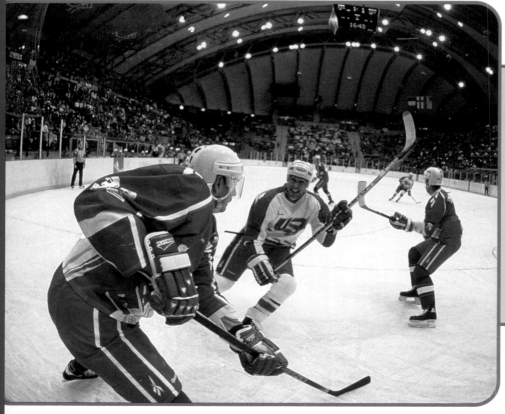

An exciting Olympic ice hockey game matched up France and the United States at the Lillehammer Winter Olympics in 1994. In the finals, Sweden beat Canada to win the gold medal.

Snow and ice

Far fewer countries send teams to the Winter Games than to the Summer Games. Countries with warm climates rarely construct ice rinks in which to train future champions. But at Albertville in 1992, there was, believe it or not, a four-man bobsled team from Jamaica! The mountainous countries of Europe have dominated the vast majority of the eighteen Winter Games. Norway, the **USSR**, Sweden, Switzerland, and Germany have been especially successful.

Often the Winter Olympians have to compete against the weather as well as against one another. Rain, thaw, blizzard, and gale have all created problems. In 1964 at Innsbruck, after a very mild winter, there was simply not enough snow for the Alpine skiing events. Austrian troops transported more than 25,000 tons of snow from higher snowfields to the River Inn Valley.

Alpine skiing for both men and women is divided into five separate events: downhill, slalom, giant slalom, super giant slalom and alpine combination (downhill and slalom). Shown here is Luxembourg's Marc Girardelli as he competes in the downhill at the Lillehammer Winter Olympics.

SPORTS FEATURED AT THE NAGANO WINTER OLYMPICS OF 1998

Alpine Skiing
Biathlon
Bobsledding
Curling
Figure Skating
Freestyle Skiing

Ice Hockey
Luge
Nordic Skiing
Ski Jumping
Snowboarding
Speed Skating

Glossary

amateur someone who competes for fun, rather than as a job, and who is unpaid

apartheid former South African political policy of keeping black people apart from white people

aristocrat a member of the upper or privileged classes

boycott to refuse to have anything to do with a person, country, or event

Cold War period after World War II of unfriendly relations between the United States and the USSR that never quite became real warfare

commercialization attempt to make money from something

communist having to do with the Communist party, which supports the idea of an economic and social system that has state-owned land, factories, and means of production. The USSR became the first Communist state in 1917. After World War II, the USSR introduced Communism into much of eastern Europe.

defect leave one country to live in another without official permission

delegate someone sent to a meeting as a representative for another person or for a group of people

eco-friendly in harmony with the natural environment

equestrianism riding or performing on horseback

landfill area of land filled in by trash or waste material

multicultural having to do with people who come from different countries and have different ideas

Nazi member or supporter of the National Socialist German Workers' Party, a political party led by Adolf Hitler in the 1930s and 1940s

pentathlon athletic contest in which a competitor takes part in five different events

professional a paid competitor

public school (in Britain) school that charges fees to attend

reclaim make land useful or productive

taxpayer person who pays a portion of their earnings to the government to pay for the running of the country

terrorist someone who uses violence to force a government to do what he or she wants

track and field sporting events that involve running, jumping, throwing, and walking, such as the 100-meter run or the javelin throw

truce temporary halting of a war or fight

USSR a communist country that included Russia and other nations that divided into separate nations in 1991

More Books to Read

Anderson, Dave. *The Story of the Olympics*. New York: Morrow, William & Company, 1996.

Dheensaw, Cleve, and Deanna Binder. *Celebrate the Spirit: The Olympic Games*. Custer, Wash.: Orca Book Publishers, 1996.

Kristy, Davida. *Coubertin's Olympics: How the Games Began*. Minneapolis: The Lerner Publishing Group, 1995.

Tames, Richard. *The Modern Olympics*. Chicago, Ill.: Heinemann Library, 1998.

Index